Dear Reader,

Wildflowers are among nature's most beautiful creations. Their brilliant colors decorate the earth, and their fragrance fills the air. I marvel at their toughness. No one takes care of them, yet somehow they reappear every spring and bring beauty to the world.

If you love wildflowers too, learn how to collect and preserve them and how to tell one flower from another. Mount them in the pages of this album and write your thoughts alongside. It will be like keeping a piece of that day, and years from now, when you look through this book, you will remember the moment you found that flower and how you felt that day.

Rona Beame

Wildflowers

A COLLECTOR'S ALBUM

By Rona Beame

Illustrated by

Dianne McElwain

RANDOM HOUSE 🏠 NEW YORK

Many thanks to James Grimes
of the New York Botanical Garden for his invaluable help.

For my three joyous children—Andrew, Richard, and Julia—and
my friends Kathy Strickland and Neila Fisher, who are always there.

Text copyright © 1994 by Rona Beame.
Illustrations copyright © 1994 by Dianne McElwain.

ISBN 0-679-81968-1

Manufactured in Singapore   1 2 3 4 5 6 7 8 9 10

Contents

Silhouettes

A New Way to Look at Flowers

Flowers can be grouped according to how and where their blossoms grow along the stem. Squint your eyes and look at the silhouette, or outline shape, of a flower and the stem that bears it. You will find that almost all flowers match one of these five basic silhouettes:

Single Flower

Each flower grows on its own stalk from a node—the place on a stem where a leaf or a branch is attached. Sometimes nodes look like small bumps.

node

Long Cluster

On a long cluster the flowers grow up and down the stalk.

Rounded Cluster

The flowers are gathered together at the top of the stalk in round or flat-topped clusters.

6

Composite Cluster

Composite flowers, such as daisies, look like a single flower but are really clusters. Each petal and each dot in the center is actually an individual flower.

Hooded Cluster

Hooded clusters also masquerade as single flowers. What looks like a large petal is really a specialized leaf that encloses a long cluster of tiny flowers.

Learning these silhouettes will be like putting on magic glasses. You'll soon be able to recognize the five basic shapes as well as subgroups within each shape. You will be able to see, for example, that the petals of a single flower can be either separate or united, or that on some long clusters the flowers don't have individual stalks but are attached directly to the central stalk.

When you collect flowers for your album, it isn't necessary to find a specific flower, like a harebell. Look for a flower with the same silhouette—a single flower with united petals. Wherever you live, you'll be able to find most of the shapes described in this book.

The Parts of a Flower

Every part of a flowering plant has one of two jobs—making seeds or feeding the plant. The flowers are in charge of making seeds and creating new plants; the roots, stem, and leaves not only make the food but also transport and store it.

pistil · *stigma* · *style* · *pollen* · *anther* · *stamen* · *sepal* · *petal* · *ovule* · *ovary*

Making Seeds

Most flowers have both male and female organs, or parts. The male organs, called the *stamens,* are found just inside the *petals.* The top parts of the stamens, called the *anthers,* are filled with *pollen,* or sperm. To make seeds, pollen must travel to a similar flower and land on the *pistil*—the female organ.

Some pollen is light enough to travel on the wind; sticky, heavier pollen is transported by insects, birds, bats, and other animals. When these animals feed on nectar (the sweet liquid a flower manufactures), they brush against the pollen and some of it clings to their body. When the animal travels to another flower, the pollen rubs off onto the *stigma* at the top of the pistil. From there it travels down the *style* and into the *ovary,* where it joins with and fertilizes an *ovule,* or egg, to make a seed.

As the seed grows, the ovary often swells to become a fruit, such as a berry or a seedpod. The petals wither, and the *sepals,* which once enclosed the bud, may now fall off, wither, or close around the fruit.

Making Food

Plants make food through a process called photosynthesis. The roots absorb water and minerals from the soil and turn it into sap. The sap travels up the stem and into the leaves, where photosynthesis takes place. In photosynthesis, plants use energy from the sun to combine water and minerals in the sap with carbon dioxide (a gas in the air) to make sugars that feed the entire plant. Because all life on earth depends on plants for food, photosynthesis is the most important process on earth.

Favorite Stopovers

The shape of a flower often determines who will come to visit. For example, the nectar in trumpet-shaped flowers is so deep inside that only insects with long tongues can reach it. Butterflies and moths are just right for the job—their tongues are often as long as their bodies! With flowers like toadflax, it takes a bumblebee or another heavy insect to push open the petals enclosing the stamens and pistil.

Sometimes the design of a flower makes life easier for insects. The largest petal on an irregularly shaped flower serves as a landing platform for insects.

Color also determines which insects will stop by for a drink. Butterflies like flowers with bright colors, especially red. Bees favor blue, while moths and other night-flying insects are attracted to white flowers glimmering in the twilight or moonlight. Petals can also have stripes and spots, known as "honey guides," which act as signposts, directing insects to the nectar.

Clusters are practical. Insects get to feast on many flowers without having to leave the premises.

Smell is important, too. The scent of roses or violets is wonderful for perfumes, but its real purpose is to attract flying visitors. Night bloomers, like honeysuckle, give off a lush, strong scent to attract moths, which can follow a smell from far away. Some wildflowers advertise their wares with putrid odors; the skunk cabbage, for instance, attracts flies with a smell like that of decaying flesh. (Fortunately there isn't a perfume called "Skunk Cabbage"!)

Collecting Wildflowers

No matter where you hunt, you'll find a wildflower waiting; whether it's Queen Anne's lace along a country roadside, bloodroot in the woods, or goldenrod growing bravely in a vacant lot. To make your search successful, here's a checklist of the things you will need:

Small scissors
Marble composition book
    (or any hardcover notebook)
Cellophane or masking tape
Pen or pencil

Always use scissors to cut a flower—don't break it off or pull it up by the roots. Cut gently, and leave a few inches of stem and some leaves. (Be careful—some flowers have sharp or pointed parts.) Place each flower carefully on its own page in the notebook. Gently tape the stem to the page so the flower does not curl up or fall out before you get home.

Write down the basic facts about each flower in your notebook—the date and place where you found it, and any special features, such as an interesting smell or hairy leaves. Number the page, and use that number later to identify the flower while it is being pressed. Otherwise you may forget what information belongs to which flower.

Midday is the best time to collect wildflowers. Wait two days after a rain, and don't collect flowers with dew on them (if there is dew, blot it gently with a paper towel when you get home; otherwise the flowers will get moldy). To protect against ticks, wear a long-sleeved shirt and long pants. Tuck the pants into your socks. Kids, take a friend along, and always tell a grown-up where you're going.

On the following pages you'll find out how to press your wildflowers and mount them in this album.

Remember, you don't have to find the exact flowers mentioned in this book—just look for similar shapes. Gather the flowers that please and interest you. The odder the better—you can puzzle out their shapes later.

Pressing Your Wildflowers

Dried flowers have their own special beauty. Unlike cut fresh flowers, they can last for years because all the moisture has been removed. One of the easiest ways to dry flowers is to press them.

You will need:

Scissors

Flowers

Blotting paper or newspapers

Heavy books or six-packs of soda

Pen or crayon

Corrugated cardboard

1.   Place flowers between 2 pieces of blotting paper or 10 sheets of newspaper (5 sheets on the bottom and 5 on top). You can put several flowers in one layer; just make sure the flowers don't touch. Don't use the color sections of a newspaper—the ink will stain the flowers.

Note: Daisies and other flowers with separate petals can be pressed "face up." Do the same for clusters like Queen Anne's lace. If the clusters are crowded, carefully cut off some of the flowers

and press them separately. With thick flowers, like thistles, slice them in half lengthwise with a sharp knife (kids, get an adult's help with the knife). Press the halves separately.

2.   Write the notebook page number on the newspaper next to each flower, so that later you can find the notes that belong to it.

3.   Place a piece of corrugated cardboard over the newspaper. If you have more flowers to press, add layers of newspaper and cardboard as needed (corrugated cardboard allows air to circulate through the pile).

4.   Top with books. Note the date somewhere on the pile.

5.   Keep your "flower press" in a warm, dry room for 3 weeks, then remove the books and gently separate the flowers from the newspaper. If the flowers feel stiff and dry, they are ready. Keep track of each flower's number (or keep each flower in the press until you are ready to mount it).

Mounting Your Wildflowers in This Album

You'll need Elmer's glue (that's what botanists use!), cardboard, tweezers, and a small paintbrush.

1.   Find the page with similarly shaped flowers.

2.   Squeeze glue onto the cardboard—not onto the flower. Lift the flower with the tweezers; put glue on the underside with the paintbrush handle. Place the flower on the mounting page; press down gently.

With delicate flowers, put glue directly on the page and let it dry a bit. Then carefully lift the flower with a moistened fingertip (use a bowl of water, not your mouth!) and place it on the glued area. Follow these steps for each flower that belongs on that page.

3.   Let the glue dry for 30 minutes before going on to another page. While you're waiting, transfer the information on the flowers you've just glued down from your field notebook to this album.

The Wildflower Collector's Code

Never pick endangered species, such as orchids, gentians, or lilies. You can write to the National Wildflower Research Center, 2600 FM 973 North, Austin, TX 78725, and ask how to get a list of endangered plants in your area.

Botanists suggest "The Rule of 20"—if you have doubts about picking a flower, make sure there are 20 of the same flower growing in the area.

Never pick anything in a nature preserve.

Never pick flowers on anyone's property without permission.

Never disturb feeding insects, especially bees. It's not wise to make stinging insects angry.

Never pull a flower up by its roots.

Never take more than you want to press at one time.

Never, _ever_ eat any part of a flower, unless you are certain it is safe. Many leaves, stems, and berries are poisonous, and the sap of some flowers can irritate your skin and eyes. Handle every flower with care.

Now turn the page and get ready for a wonderful adventure!

Single Flowers

One flower grows on its own stalk from each node.

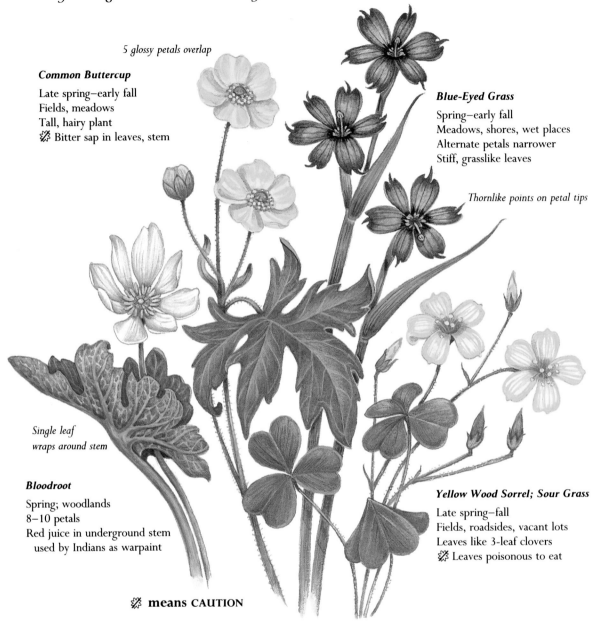

5 glossy petals overlap

Common Buttercup

Late spring–early fall
Fields, meadows
Tall, hairy plant
�֍ Bitter sap in leaves, stem

Blue-Eyed Grass

Spring–early fall
Meadows, shores, wet places
Alternate petals narrower
Stiff, grasslike leaves

Thornlike points on petal tips

*Single leaf
wraps around stem*

Bloodroot

Spring; woodlands
8–10 petals
Red juice in underground stem
 used by Indians as warpaint

Yellow Wood Sorrel; Sour Grass

Late spring–fall
Fields, roadsides, vacant lots
Leaves like 3-leaf clovers
✖ Leaves poisonous to eat

✖ **means CAUTION**

Separate Petals

Petals are completely separate from one another. Look for five petals, but there can be 3, 4, 6, or more. The blossom has a wheel shape (blue-eyed grass) or saucer shape (buttercup).

*Bloodroot closes up tight at night. In the
morning the petals unfold in the sunlight.*

Single Flowers

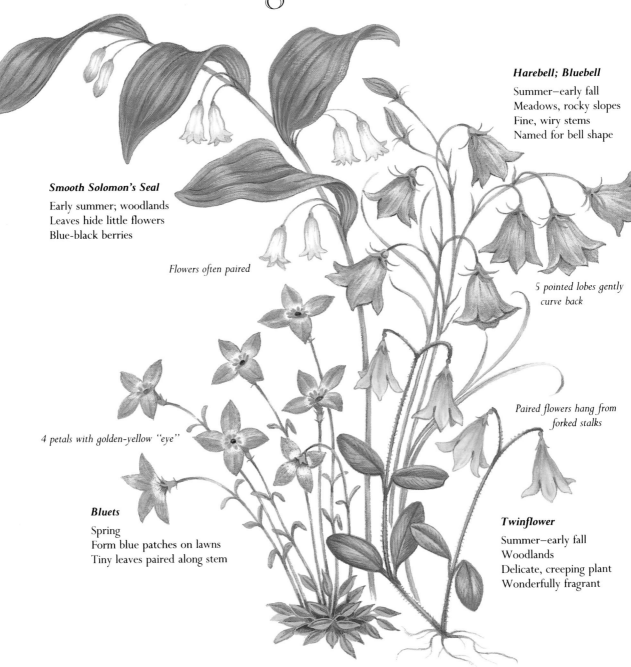

Harebell; Bluebell

Summer–early fall
Meadows, rocky slopes
Fine, wiry stems
Named for bell shape

Smooth Solomon's Seal

Early summer; woodlands
Leaves hide little flowers
Blue-black berries

Flowers often paired

5 pointed lobes gently curve back

4 petals with golden-yellow "eye"

Paired flowers hang from forked stalks

Bluets

Spring
Form blue patches on lawns
Tiny leaves paired along stem

Twinflower

Summer–early fall
Woodlands
Delicate, creeping plant
Wonderfully fragrant

United Petals

Petals join to form a tube. They can be joined at the base only (bluets), or almost totally with just the lobes, or tips of the petals, separate (harebell). Flowers with united petals can be shaped like bells, funnels, or bowls.

Moths hover in front of a flower as they drink its nectar; butterflies always drink sitting on a flower's petals.

21

Single Flowers

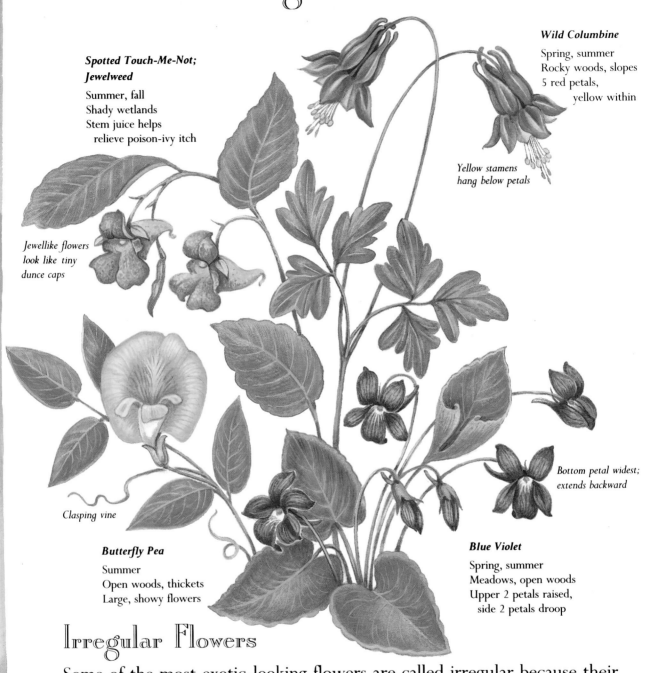

Spotted Touch-Me-Not; Jewelweed

Summer, fall
Shady wetlands
Stem juice helps
relieve poison-ivy itch

Jewellike flowers look like tiny dunce caps

Wild Columbine

Spring, summer
Rocky woods, slopes
5 red petals,
yellow within

Yellow stamens hang below petals

Clasping vine

Butterfly Pea

Summer
Open woods, thickets
Large, showy flowers

Bottom petal widest; extends backward

Blue Violet

Spring, summer
Meadows, open woods
Upper 2 petals raised,
side 2 petals droop

Irregular Flowers

Some of the most exotic-looking flowers are called irregular because their petals are not all the same shape. The differences may be minor, like the slightly different-sized petals of the blue violet, or more extreme, like the petals of the lovely spotted touch-me-not, which differ in size and are both united and separate.

Like moths, hummingbirds drink while hovering in front of a flower. Spotted touch-me-not is one of their favorites. The ripe pods of this flower explode when touched.

Long Clusters

Long clusters are tall and skinny, with flowers growing all along the stalk. Clusters are very economical; one set of roots, stems, and leaves provides for a lot of flowers.

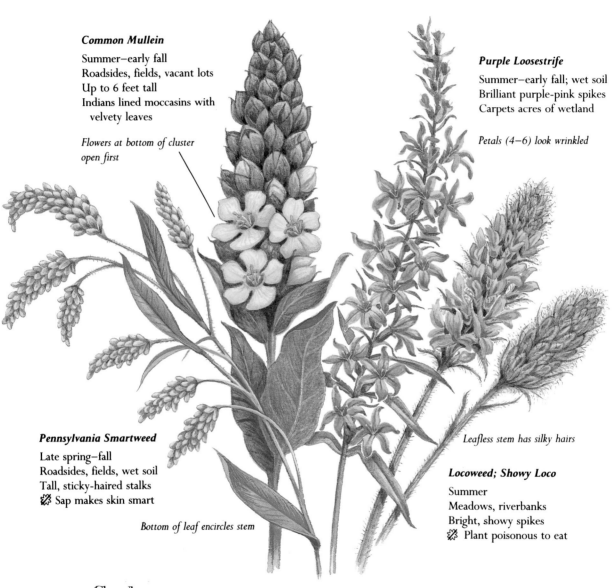

Common Mullein

Summer–early fall
Roadsides, fields, vacant lots
Up to 6 feet tall
Indians lined moccasins with
velvety leaves

Flowers at bottom of cluster open first

Purple Loosestrife

Summer–early fall; wet soil
Brilliant purple-pink spikes
Carpets acres of wetland

Petals (4–6) look wrinkled

Leafless stem has silky hairs

Pennsylvania Smartweed

Late spring–fall
Roadsides, fields, wet soil
Tall, sticky-haired stalks
❀ Sap makes skin smart

Bottom of leaf encircles stem

Locoweed; Showy Loco

Summer
Meadows, riverbanks
Bright, showy spikes
❀ Plant poisonous to eat

Spikes

The flowers on a spike cluster do not have small stalks, but are attached directly to the large central stalk. The spikes can be small and delicate (Pennsylvania smartweed) or very large (common mullein).

Butterflies use their antenna to smell, but taste
with their feet. The hairs on the bottom of
their feet are taste organs.

25

Long Clusters

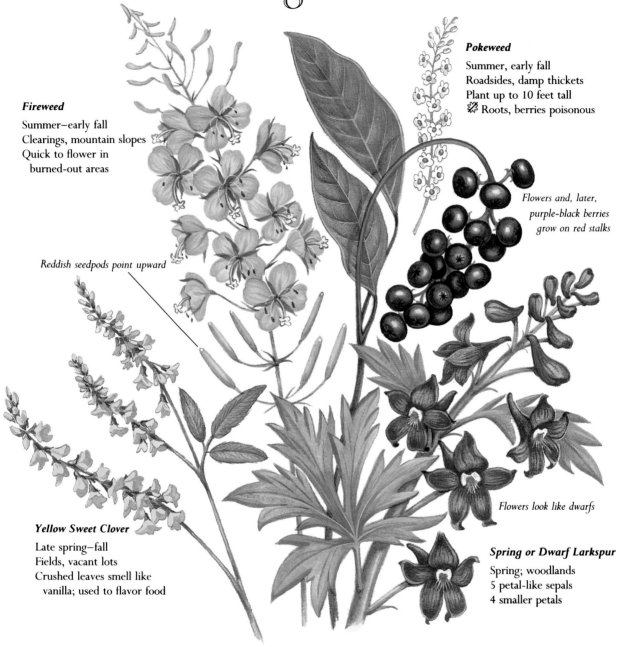

Fireweed

Summer–early fall
Clearings, mountain slopes
Quick to flower in
  burned-out areas

Pokeweed

Summer, early fall
Roadsides, damp thickets
Plant up to 10 feet tall
☠ Roots, berries poisonous

*Flowers and, later,
purple-black berries
grow on red stalks*

Reddish seedpods point upward

Flowers look like dwarfs

Yellow Sweet Clover

Late spring–fall
Fields, vacant lots
Crushed leaves smell like
  vanilla; used to flavor food

Spring or Dwarf Larkspur

Spring; woodlands
5 petal-like sepals
4 smaller petals

Racemes

The flowers on a raceme cluster grow on tiny individual stalks that are attached to a main stalk.

Grouse and other game birds like the seeds of yellow sweet clover.

Long Clusters

Featherbells
Summer, early fall
Woodlands, thickets
Feathery cluster
Flowers look like
    pointy stars

*Grasslike leaves
folded lengthwise*

Steeplebush
Late summer, early fall
Fields, meadows
Fuzzy, steeple-shaped cluster
Blossoms at top open first

False Solomon's Seal
Spring, summer; woodlands
Leaves dwarf tiny flowers
Pale berries turn bright red

Flowers look like jacks

Goatsbeard
Late spring, summer
Woods; deep, narrow valleys
Plant up to 6 feet tall

*Underside of steeplebush leaves
woolly, brownish yellow*

Panicles

On a panicle cluster, branches grow from a central stalk, and flowers grow along the branches.

Cut-leafed toothwort

Trout lily

You'll find that most wildflowers are white or yellow.

Rounded Clusters

Bunched together toward the top of the stalk, the flowers of rounded-cluster plants can range from ball-shaped (garden phlox) to flat-topped (Queen Anne's lace; next page).

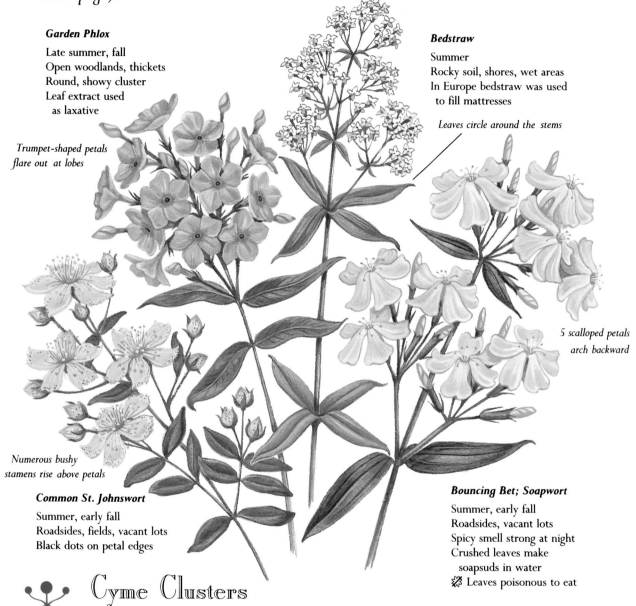

Garden Phlox

Late summer, fall
Open woodlands, thickets
Round, showy cluster
Leaf extract used
   as laxative

*Trumpet-shaped petals
flare out at lobes*

Bedstraw

Summer
Rocky soil, shores, wet areas
In Europe bedstraw was used
   to fill mattresses

Leaves circle around the stems

*5 scalloped petals
arch backward*

*Numerous bushy
stamens rise above petals*

Common St. Johnswort

Summer, early fall
Roadsides, fields, vacant lots
Black dots on petal edges

Bouncing Bet; Soapwort

Summer, early fall
Roadsides, vacant lots
Spicy smell strong at night
Crushed leaves make
   soapsuds in water
❈ Leaves poisonous to eat

Cyme Clusters

The branches on cyme clusters grow opposite each other on the stem. The flowers grow in groups of threes; the middle flower blooms first.

There are faint dots on the leaves of the common St. Johnswort—hold the leaves up to the light to see the dots.

Rounded Clusters

Common Milkweed

Summer;
  roadsides, vacant lots
Milky juice inside stem, leaves

Milkweed fruit pods look like they have warts

Queen Anne's Lace; Wild Carrot

Late spring–fall
Roadsides, fields, vacant lots
Purple flower in center
Ancestor of garden carrot

Old umbels curl up like birds' nests

Golden Alexanders

Spring; meadows, moist areas
Flat, loose cluster
Member of parsley family

Cow Parsnip

Summer; moist ground
Up to 10 feet tall
Unpleasant smell

Ridged, fuzzy stem

Umbels

Umbels look like umbrellas. All the individual flower stalks radiate from the same point. When the outer stalks are longest, the cluster is flat on top. Some umbels, such as common milkweed, have only one flower on each stalk. Others—such as cow parsnip and golden alexanders—have a miniature umbel cluster on the end of each stalk.

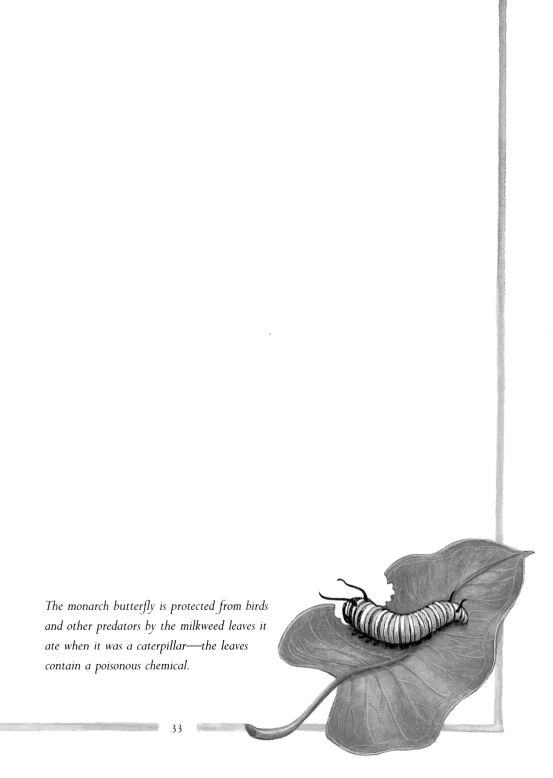

The monarch butterfly is protected from birds and other predators by the milkweed leaves it ate when it was a caterpillar—the leaves contain a poisonous chemical.

Composite Clusters

In composite wildflowers, blossoms are clustered together in miniature bouquets that masquerade as single flowers. Within the cluster there may be two kinds of flowers: "disk" flowers, which have united petals and look like little tubes; and "ray" flowers, which look like one long petal.

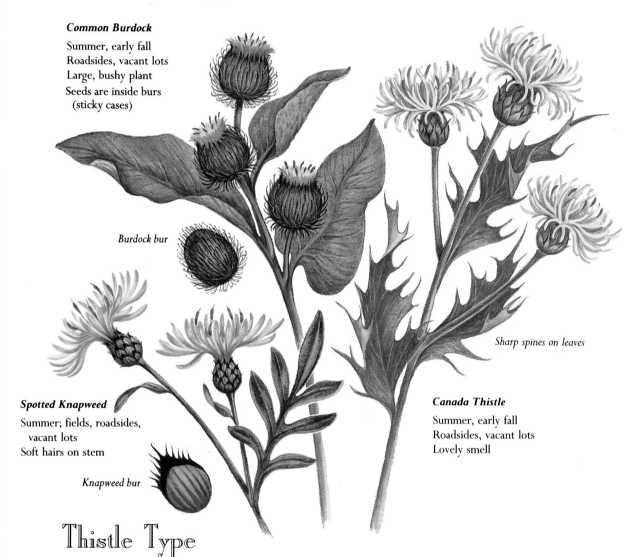

Common Burdock
Summer, early fall
Roadsides, vacant lots
Large, bushy plant
Seeds are inside burs
 (sticky cases)

Burdock bur

Sharp spines on leaves

Spotted Knapweed
Summer; fields, roadsides,
 vacant lots
Soft hairs on stem

Knapweed bur

Canada Thistle
Summer, early fall
Roadsides, vacant lots
Lovely smell

Thistle Type

Thistle-type flowerheads are packed tight with tiny, tube-shaped disk flowers. Each disk flower has five lobes that surround the taller stamen and stigma. There are no ray flowers.

The sticky burs of the common burdock catch onto clothing and the fur of animals. The burs can travel for miles before the animal scratches or rubs them off.

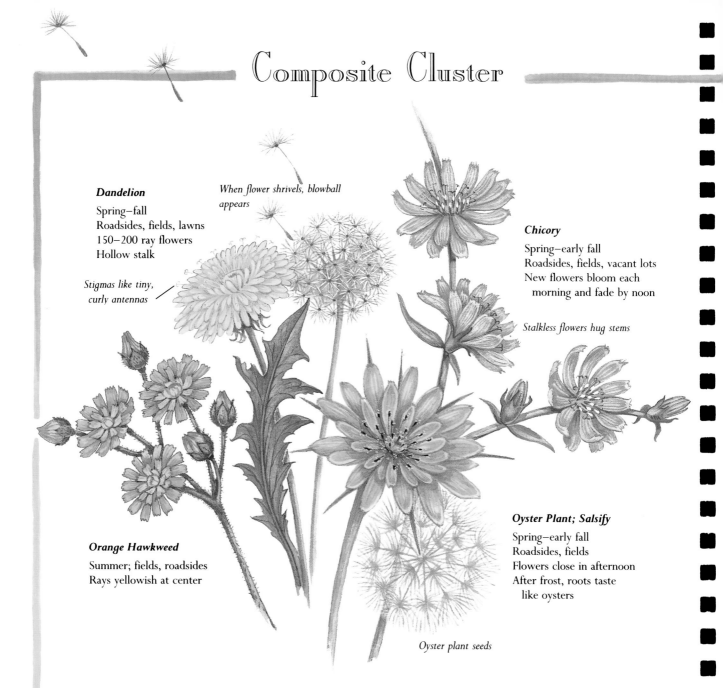

Dandelion
Spring–fall
Roadsides, fields, lawns
150–200 ray flowers
Hollow stalk

*Stigmas like tiny,
curly antennas*

*When flower shrivels, blowball
appears*

Chicory
Spring–early fall
Roadsides, fields, vacant lots
New flowers bloom each
    morning and fade by noon

Stalkless flowers hug stems

Oyster Plant; Salsify
Spring–early fall
Roadsides, fields
Flowers close in afternoon
After frost, roots taste
    like oysters

Orange Hawkweed
Summer; fields, roadsides
Rays yellowish at center

Oyster plant seeds

Dandelion Type

Dandelion-type flowerheads are made up of tiny ray flowers. A close look
at the tip of a ray flower reveals the tiny pointed ends of five petals united
into one. Often the tips are squared off.

A wildflower is considered a weed when it gets in someone's way. When dandelions carpet an empty field with gold, people think they're beautiful. But let them grow on someone's front lawn, and they become a nuisance.

Composite Cluster

Black-Eyed Susan

Summer, early fall
Fields, roadsides,
   vacant lots
Leaves and stem hairy

*Disk sticks out
like a button*

Common Sunflower

Summer, fall; prairies,
   roadsides, vacant lots
Flowers 6 inches wide

Disk lowest in center

Many fringelike rays

Common Fleabane

Spring, summer
Fields, thickets, open woods
Disks resemble yolk of egg
Fleas hate the oil in leaves

Oxeye Daisy

Late spring–early fall
Roadsides, vacant lots
Dark-green toothed leaves
"Day's eye" closes at dusk
Gives cow's milk a
   funny taste

Daisy Type

Daisy-type flowerheads have both ray and disk flowers. Their centers are crammed with tube-shaped disk flowers, which are encircled by showier ray flowers—usually of a different color. In many daisy types, like the sunflower, only the disk flowers are fertile and can produce seeds. The ray flowers are infertile and cannot produce seeds.

Most birds love sunflower seeds, which come from the disk of the flower. Unfortunately for birds, squirrels love the seeds, too, and they are geniuses at getting into birdfeeders.

Composite Clusters

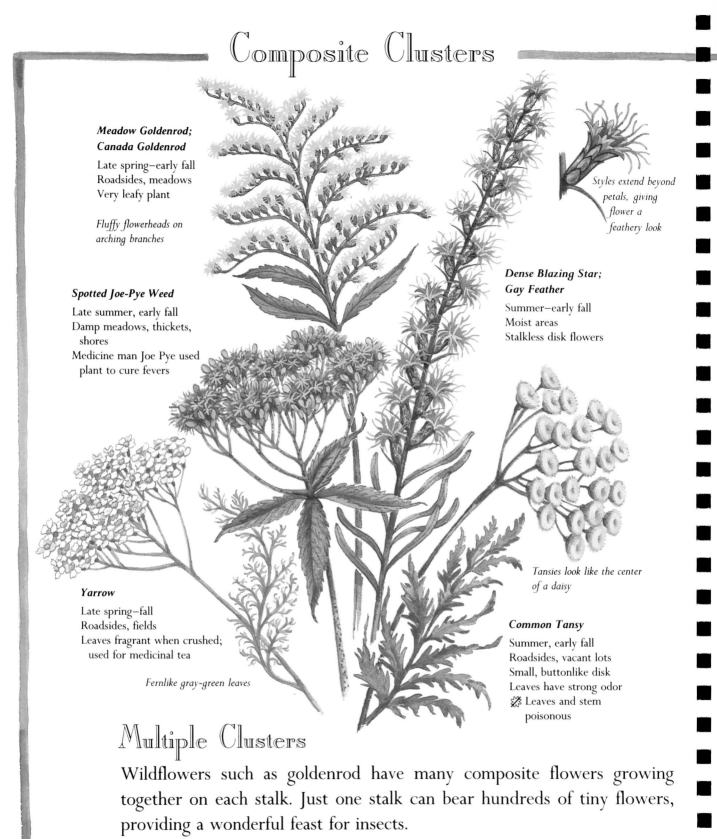

**Meadow Goldenrod;
Canada Goldenrod**

Late spring–early fall
Roadsides, meadows
Very leafy plant

*Fluffy flowerheads on
arching branches*

Spotted Joe-Pye Weed

Late summer, early fall
Damp meadows, thickets,
  shores
Medicine man Joe Pye used
  plant to cure fevers

*Styles extend beyond
petals, giving
flower a
feathery look*

**Dense Blazing Star;
Gay Feather**

Summer–early fall
Moist areas
Stalkless disk flowers

Yarrow

Late spring–fall
Roadsides, fields
Leaves fragrant when crushed;
  used for medicinal tea

Fernlike gray-green leaves

*Tansies look like the center
of a daisy*

Common Tansy

Summer, early fall
Roadsides, vacant lots
Small, buttonlike disk
Leaves have strong odor
❊ Leaves and stem
  poisonous

Multiple Clusters

Wildflowers such as goldenrod have many composite flowers growing together on each stalk. Just one stalk can bear hundreds of tiny flowers, providing a wonderful feast for insects.

Woodland flowers are native Americans. The
wildflowers that grow on roadsides and in
vacant lots, however, such as tansies, were
brought here by European settlers. Often the
seeds were stowaways in a coat pocket, a straw
mattress, or the heel of a shoe.

Hooded Clusters

This group includes some strange-looking flowers. Most have a spathe, which looks like a large, showy petal but is actually a specialized leaf. Hoodlike, the spathe surrounds a spike, or spadix, which is crowded with tiny flowers.

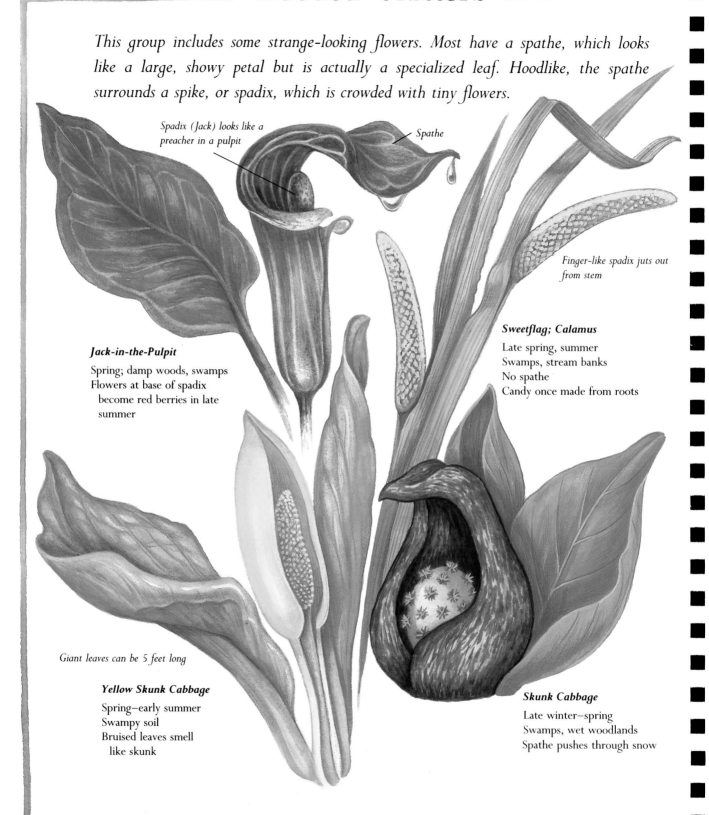

Spadix (Jack) looks like a preacher in a pulpit

Spathe

Finger-like spadix juts out from stem

Jack-in-the-Pulpit

Spring; damp woods, swamps
Flowers at base of spadix
  become red berries in late
  summer

Sweetflag; Calamus

Late spring, summer
Swamps, stream banks
No spathe
Candy once made from roots

Giant leaves can be 5 feet long

Yellow Skunk Cabbage

Spring–early summer
Swampy soil
Bruised leaves smell
  like skunk

Skunk Cabbage

Late winter–spring
Swamps, wet woodlands
Spathe pushes through snow

The skunk cabbage creates its own heat (up to 72°F) and can use this heat to push its way up through snow in winter.

The Forgotten Wildflowers

This page is dedicated to the plain-looking wildflowers no one notices—grasses, rushes, plantains, and ragweeds. Most are wind-pollinated. Their tiny flowers have either small petals or tough bracts. (Bracts, which look like small green leaves, protect the flower's reproductive parts.) Though most are long clusters, they have their own page in this album so that you will look for them, collect them, and think of them as wildflowers too

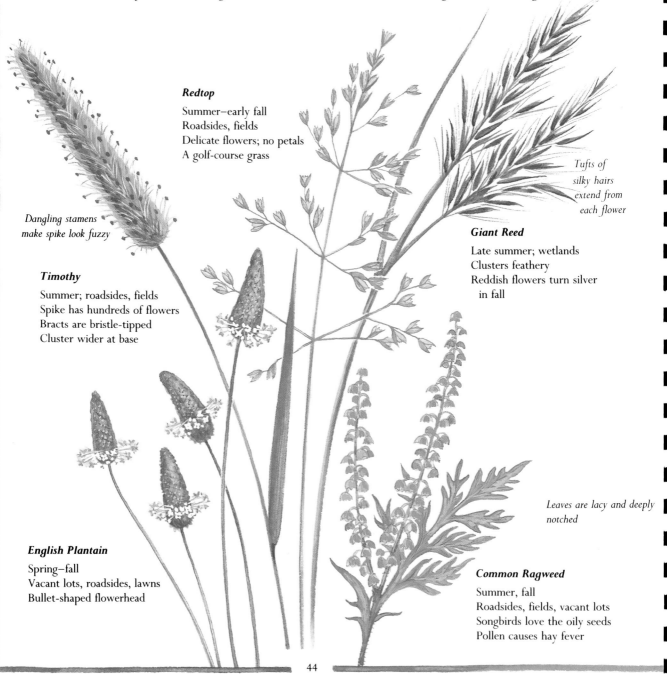

Redtop
Summer–early fall
Roadsides, fields
Delicate flowers; no petals
A golf-course grass

Tufts of silky hairs extend from each flower

Dangling stamens make spike look fuzzy

Giant Reed
Late summer; wetlands
Clusters feathery
Reddish flowers turn silver
 in fall

Timothy
Summer; roadsides, fields
Spike has hundreds of flowers
Bracts are bristle-tipped
Cluster wider at base

Leaves are lacy and deeply notched

English Plantain
Spring–fall
Vacant lots, roadsides, lawns
Bullet-shaped flowerhead

Common Ragweed
Summer, fall
Roadsides, fields, vacant lots
Songbirds love the oily seeds
Pollen causes hay fever

Gardeners are not happy when English plantain pops up on their lawns. But songbirds love the seeds, and the leaves are a rabbit's favorite meal.

Flower Postcards, Bookmarks, and Stationery

It's almost magical the way an ordinary piece of paper is transformed into something beautiful the minute you place a pressed flower on it. Here's a way to make postcards, bookmarks, and stationery for yourself or as gifts for friends and family.

You will need:

Ruler

Pencil

Unlined index cards

Postage stamps

Scissors

Clear contact paper

Pressed flowers and leaves

*Colored notepaper
    and matching envelopes*

*Colored construction paper
    or fabric (optional)*

Elmer's glue

Postcards

1.   Using the ruler, draw a line down the middle of an index card. Write a message on the left side; on the right, put a stamp and a friend's name and address.

2.   Turn the card over and arrange flowers and leaves in a design you like. Be creative—mix colors and shapes. Put a dab of glue under each flower to hold it lightly in place on the card.

3.   Cut a piece of contact paper slightly larger than the card. Peel off the backing and lay the contact paper over the flowers. Starting from the center, gently press out any wrinkles or air bubbles. To get rid of big wrinkles, lift the contact paper on that side and then press it down again. Trim the excess contact paper.

Contact paper slightly larger than card

Bookmarks and Stationery

To make bookmarks, follow the same steps, but cut your index card in half lengthwise.

For stationery, fold a sheet of notepaper in half. Place flowers directly on one of the outside halves and then cover with contact paper. To decorate your notepaper with appliqués, cut out a small piece of colored paper or fabric, place a flower on top, and cover both with contact paper. Then cut the appliqué into any shape, such as a heart or a diamond, and glue it to the notepaper.

Flower Pals

Do you have a pen pal? Why not exchange flowers through the mail with him or her and become "flower pals"?

Mail only pressed flowers to each other, and put them between protective layers of cardboard. It's a great way to learn about flowers from different parts of the country—and the world!

Flower Perfume

Most perfumes have an alcohol base, but you can make your own flower perfume with this recipe, which uses oil instead. If you can't find flowers in the wild with a smell you like, ask a florist for some fragrant flowers that are imperfect and not too expensive.

You will need:

14 ounces of any <u>odorless</u> oil, such as mineral, cottonseed, or safflower

Bowl large enough to hold the oil

Scissors

Small roll of sterilized cotton

Wide-mouthed ceramic or glass jar with lid

Fresh petals from 12 fragrant flowers

<u>Un-iodized</u> table salt (do not use iodized salt)

Clean, heavy rock or paperweight

Masking tape

Cheesecloth

16-ounce measuring cup with pouring spout

Small funnel

Perfume bottle with tight stopper

1.   Pour the oil into the bowl. Cut a piece of cotton to cover the bottom of the jar, doubling it until it is an inch thick. Soak the cotton pad in the oil and place it in the jar.

2.   Place an inch-thick layer of petals over the cotton and sprinkle with salt. Don't cover the petals completely; just sprinkle enough so you can see the salt.

3.   Add more layers of inch-thick, oil-soaked cotton, petals, and salt until the jar is three-quarters full. Make sure the cotton always covers all the petals and touches the sides of the jar. Add a final layer of cotton. Put the rock on top and press down firmly. Leave the rock in the jar, put the lid on, and seal with masking tape. Let sit for 48 hours.

4.   Open the jar. Remove the cotton, place it in the cheesecloth, and squeeze the perfumed oil into the measuring cup. Slowly pour the oil through the funnel into the perfume bottle. Don't leave your perfume exposed to the air; always store it in a stoppered bottle.

Flower Paintings

With some inexpensive frames and a little imagination, even a beginner can create wonderful flower "paintings" to enrich any room.

You will need:

Picture frame with glass	*Elmer's glue*	*Cotton swab*
Pencil	*Tweezers*	*Heavy books*
Posterboard or other heavy paper	*Toothpicks*	*Paper towels*
Scissors	*Cardboard*	*Pressed flowers, stems,*
Black velvet or felt	*Glass cleaner*	*leaves, ferns, grasses*

1.   Remove the glass from the frame (kids, get an adult to help you). Trace the outline of the glass onto the posterboard and cut out this shape. If you want a velvet or felt background: Using the posterboard as a pattern, cut a piece of velvet one inch larger all around. Wrap the velvet around the posterboard and glue it to the back.

2.   With the tweezers, start placing flowers on the posterboard. First select the flower or flowers that will be the "focal point" of your painting—the place for the eye to focus on. This is the most important spot in any picture. It could be the biggest flower or the brightest color.

3.   Choose slender grasses to create 3 graceful, curving lines of different heights that will lead the eye to the focal point. Add flowers and move them around until the design pleases you.

4.   Put some glue on a piece of cardboard. Lift each flower with the tweezer. Use a toothpick to apply a dab of glue to the underside of a flower, and place the flower back on the posterboard. Press it down gently.

Lift more fragile flowers with a moistened fingertip and put the glue directly on the posterboard.

5.   When you have glued all the flowers down, blow gently to make sure you didn't miss any. Remove loose pieces with a moist cotton swab.

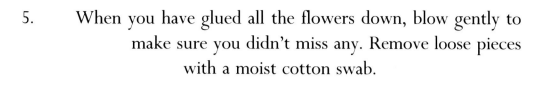

6.   Let the glue dry for two hours. Meanwhile, remove fingerprints and smudges from the glass with the glass cleaner and a paper towel.

7.   To "seal" your painting from moisture and air: Put a thin line of glue on the front outer edges of the posterboard and place the glass on top. Press the edge of the glass onto the glue. Weight the glass overnight with the books.

8.   Place the flower painting in the frame. If the fit isn't snug, add sheets of cardboard at the back.

Bright light will fade your flowers, so keep the picture away from lamps and out of direct sunlight. After this much work, you want your painting to look its best as long as possible!

How to Air-Dry Flowers

yarrow

salvia

When flowers die in the fall, some continue to look beautiful even though they've dried up. Golden- or silver-colored reeds, grasses, and dramatic-looking seedpods like milkweed can be picked in autumn and go straight from the roadside to your room with no preparation. They will last a long time.

Other wildflowers lose their beauty when they dry up outdoors naturally. Many of them make wonderful decorations if they are air-dried indoors. But you must pick them in summer, before they die. You'll find their names in the instructions below.

You will need:

Fresh flowers	*Scissors*
Vase or other large-mouthed container	*Wire coat hangers*
Pipe cleaners or string	*Shoeboxes with lids*

1.   Gather flowers to be air-dried around midday on a hot, dry day, but not so hot that petals and leaves are drooping. Choose mature, perfect blooms. Light-colored flowers seem to air-dry better. Some flowers change color as the summer progresses; pick them at the stage you like.

2.   As soon as you get home, remove the leaves and start drying the flowers. Do not place them in water.

3.   There are two ways to air-dry flowers—right-side up or upside down. Generally, heavy-headed grasses and flowers with sturdy

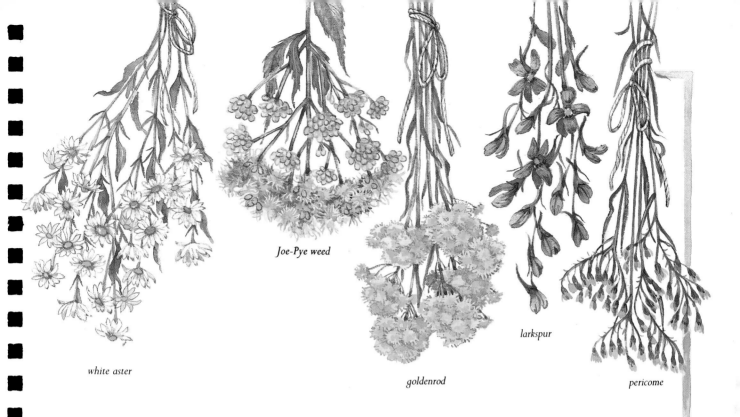

Joe-Pye weed

white aster

goldenrod

larkspur

pericome

stems and large clusters should be placed right-side up in a container and put in a closet or a warm, dark room. This group includes Queen Anne's lace, goldenrod, hydrangea, cattail (pick when green or light tan), bittersweet, and pussy willow.

4.   Flowers to be dried upside down include tansy, yarrow, white aster, larkspur, columbine, goldenrod, pericome, and Joe-Pye weed (which should be gathered in the bud stage).

Divide the flowers into bunches of four. With pipe cleaners or string, tie the stems tightly together so the flowers won't slip out as they dry. Thicker stalks can be hung separately.

5.   Tie several bunches to the bottom of a wire hanger. Cut each string a different length so each bunch has its own space. Hang from a closet rod or nail.

6.   Flowers are ready in 1 to 2 weeks, when the petals feel dry and slightly brittle. Separate each flower carefully and store in lidded boxes until you're ready to arrange them.

Arranging Dried Flowers

Dried flowers have their own special beauty and add warmth and color to a room. Choose a rainy day to work with dried flowers, because the flowers will be less brittle.

You will need:

Container with wide mouth	Dried flowers
Sand	Florist's wire
Water	Scissors
Modeling clay	Florist's tape

1. Fill the container to an inch from the top with sand to make it steady. Sprinkle just enough water over the sand to dampen the top 2 or 3 inches. Cover with a half-inch layer of clay and press the edges against the rim of the container.

2. To strengthen short or fragile stems: Lay a piece of florist's wire halfway down the stem. Wire and stem should overlap 2 inches. Wind another piece of wire around the overlap; cover it with florist's tape. If the stem is hollow, gently push a wire up inside.

3. Select the brightest, largest, or most dramatic flowers as your focal point. Put them aside to be added last.

4. Create the outline of your arrangement with tall, thin clusters and grasses. Decide where you want the highest point—generally, it should be twice the height of the container. Take your time; shift and change the design now—once you've filled in, it will be impossible.

5.   Start adding flowers from the outside in, using rounded clusters and, finally, single flowers. Use lighter colors and smaller flowers at the top, deeper shades and larger blossoms at the bottom, so your design doesn't look top-heavy. Distribute pointed and round flowers evenly throughout. Make sure stems and wires are hidden. When everything is in place, add the flowers you've chosen as the focal point.

6.   Hang a graceful or feathery flower over the side of the container to "break the line." Stand back and appreciate your first "professional" flower arrangement.

Index

Scientists give Latin names to flowers because their common names often differ in various parts of the country. Orange hawkweed, for example, is also called devil's paintbrush, but its Latin name is the same worldwide: *Hieracium aurantiacum. Hieracium,* the genus name (like "Smith"), tells us this plant is a hawkweed; *aurantiacum,* the species name (like "Richard"), tells us what kind of hawkweed it is—in this case, orange.

Below are the Latin names for each wildflower in this book, followed by abbreviations for where they grow. The meanings of the abbreviations are:

All Areas = United States, Canada

All Can = All of Canada

All US = All of United States

E = East coast of US

C = Central US

NE = Northeast US

NW = Northwest US

W = West coast of US

E Can = Eastern Canada

C Can = Central Canada

S Can = Southern Canada

W Can = Western Canada, Alaska

Next to each name you'll also find an abbreviation for the size of the flowerhead. The abbreviations mean: w. = width, for flowers with saucer shapes, such as buttercup; l. = length, for bell-like flowers (harebell)

For clusters with tiny flowers, size refers to the entire cluster: cw. = cluster width, for rounded clusters; cl. = cluster length, for long clusters